Praise for

Unabashed Truths t_____ ry Won_ _ _____ _ou

"Joann's book will save you time, money and personal distress!"
—Bob Luke, Celebrity Acting Coach, NYC/LA

A must read for anyone and everyone no matter age, location or where you are currently on the ladder of success. Anyone from novices starting out to veterans who want to reboot their careers will gain information and insight from Joann's book. Save time, heartache and money - buy and read this book immediately!
—Jacque Pedersen-Schrimscher, Talent Agent, Los Angeles/NYC/Mid-South

'Joann's guidebook is right on the mark — a succinct, honest and trustworthy view of the business of acting from an insider with a unique perspective."
—David Bellantoni, Casting Director/Writer Director, NYC/LA

"Learning from those who have jumped the hurdles of the entertainment industry Joann Perahia's testimony and guide book is drawn from real experiences. Make this book a part of your acting career action plan!"
—Megan Martin, LMSW, SAG/AFTRA, NYC

"Joann's book is an easy read with a wealth of information at your fingertips for a parent of a child actor, actor or retiree. She gives you leads and the hard-cold truths in order to navigate the industry."
—Sue Rossi, OLY, 1984 Olympics, Luge Team/ CA

Unabashed Truths
the Entertainment Industry
Won't Tell You

Unabashed Truths
the Entertainment Industry
Won't Tell You

A Guide to the Business of Acting

Joann Perahia

Dedication

To my husband, Claude Haussmann, for over three decades of bliss and unconditional love. This book would not have happened if it weren't for you and our twins, Alexandre and Philippe Haussmann. Alex and Philippe, you are my gifts and I am so proud of the extraordinary men you've become.

Acknowledgements

I would like to thank the following people who have all contributed to this book. I appreciate your knowledge, expertise, feedback and support.

Jacque Pedersen-Schrimscher, LA Talent Agent extraordinaire for more than 40 years. You helped make this book happen with your infinite knowledge and expertise. Part of the *Unabashed Truths* sisterhood.

Bob Luke, NY/LA, Celebrity Acting Coach. For your wisdom, knowledge and support. (www.boblukestudios.com).

David Bellantoni, NY Casting Director/Director/Writer. For your honesty and humor in dealing with this crazy industry.

April Bartlett, LA Talent Manager. For sharing your experiences and your knowledge of this industry from all angles. (www.bartlettcartertalent.com).

Mary Ellen Landolfi, my remarkable editor and copywriter. (www.wordspiralmedia.com).

Carol Ingaro, my incredibly talented graphic designer and cover artist. (www.ingarodesigns.com).

Kate Rafferty, SEO Expert and Marketer. Because of your suggestion, all of this came to be. Thank you so much for your expertise and kindness. (www.kateraffertyseo.com)

Contents

Introduction

The purpose of this guide is to provide the truth about a business that "has no rules." There are many books written by Agents, Casting Directors, actors, etc. With this book, I present my perspective and multi-faceted experience in the entertainment industry. I am the parent of child actors (twins and now grown) who were in feature films in their youth. I've also helped Agents and I now act in my retirement career. I am a retired IT Consultant as well as a figure skating coach. I have no vested interest, no lies — just unabashed truths. I want to give you the reality so that you have the greatest chance of success. If you want truth read on. If you don't, then close the book and unplug.

This book is for you if you fit any of the categories below:

- A parent who has a child who is interested in being a child actor (Child Actor)
- A beginning actor whether you studied fine arts or not (Beginner Actor).

- A retiree who wants to try their unspoken dream of acting and supplement their income (Retiree).

The following guide will help you navigate an industry that is unstructured, has no rules, and can set you soaring skyward or into a swift downward spiral. This book is to help guide you to discover whether or not you should embark on the acting journey and whether or not it is for you/your child. I want to help you succeed. Please note I focus on TV/Film/Commercials, not the Theatre, but it really is the same process. To this day I still say, if you want to be on stage go to NYC, if you want to be in Film/TV go to LA. However, with technology and all the new places for filming this doesn't hold as well as it did before.

You can be the "best" actor with tons of talent, or the committed parent of a talented child actor, but you also must be capable of handling the "Business" part of acting. There are two parts of acting: your *craft* and your *business*. The business side is exactly what it states. You are a commodity and you must be able to market yourself just as if you were marketing a product. In this day and age of the internet and social media, actors have to use those tools themselves. Agents and Managers do not do this for you in total. Unless maybe you are Matt Damon, who has a whole staff and pays them, hopefully very well. Additionally, as with any product, you have to network so you can get your product out there. These pages will help you.

However, you must be able to handle both. This guide was created for just that purpose. It should give you the insight as to whether this journey is for you or not. If you chose this path, whether you are a parent of a child actor, an aspiring actor or a retiree, this guide is the abridged version of what can be a rollercoaster ride.

Now, a little background about me. I always loved entertaining and the entertainment industry. I loved to sing and dance. I would organize my cousins and put on shows for my family as a child during holiday gatherings. I did attend Performing Arts camps and performed in school plays and took dancing classes in ballet and tap. I also figure skated and in fact, I am still currently a figure skating coach. But what stopped me was the "business" end of acting. In my day, the only side job was being a waitress. I am a klutz. Even though I can dance and figure skate, I can't carry plates for anything.

Instead I went to college and earned a graduate degree in Information Technology. However, the "thespian" was always in me. I spoke and presented at technology conferences and skated in local shows. As the old saying goes, if you don't like your job then do the things you love outside of work, because the bills have to get paid. So, I did what I loved in my spare time.

However, when my twins were growing up, I noticed their knack for the entertainment industry and not sports. Together we set on their path of becoming child actors. They were cast and played the Russian twins in Roland

Emmerich's film *2012*. Essentially, I became their Manager and I learned about this "business with no rules" for children, which has more twists, turns and, in reality, more rules and inequities than for an adult actor. This is why this Guide captures (where applicable) in each chapter a section for parents of actors, adult actors, and retirees. On my own journey, I assisted a Talent Agent and learned that side of the business as well.

I hope you find this guidebook helpful. There are no "Hollywood" lines in this manual. Just real direction. I've included websites and resources that you can use in order to start your journey. Please note there are many more and even as of this writing, more are created and posted on the Internet. However, the ones I have included here I consider "tried and true," and have been around for a while.

I have developed and included in this book several questionnaires aimed at the parent of a child actor, the child actor (to be answered by the parent) and the actor/retiree actor. These are upfront and candid questions for you to answer truthfully so you can determine whether this business is truly for you, or your child if that's the case. Honesty is what you need for yourself, and that's also what this guide will give you, brutally at times. Honesty so you can succeed. So, after reading this Introduction, you might want to turn to Chapter 5 and honestly answer the questions first. Then you might decide not to read the book, but you took the first step to see whether this is a "business" you can handle.

This is a great retirement career for a retiree who wants to supplement their income if they live in a filming city/state; there are many all over the country now. Now you're going to hear this from me throughout this book, but it's true — Google is your friend. I could list the cities and states but more pop up even as I type. Again, the questionnaire will determine whether it's a fit for you too.

I also wrote this book to address both the similarities and differences that will apply depending on whether you are the parent of a child actor, a regular actor (including an actor who wants to get back into the business) or a retiree who wants to act. I first cover a topic the way it applies to all and then if necessary, I will break out each specific audience – Parent of Child Actor, Regular Actor, and Retiree, to address and describe the differences. If it is not broken out, then there are no differences.

Please visit my website (www.joannperahia.com) for updates, news and other information. Remember, have fun because life is short, or as they say, "Life is like a toilet paper roll, it goes faster in the end." Good luck with your journey.

Joann Perahia
April 2019

Chapter 1 – Prepare

Whether you are the parent of a child actor, an actor, or a retiree actor *you have to prepare!* The preparation is definitely a bit different for each category of actor, so I will state the generalities and give the details for each. However, I have put them in what I believe is the order of priority and what worked for us.

- Acting Classes
- Headshots
- Resume

Acting Classes

Acting classes are essential. These classes will enhance your self-esteem, self-confidence and ability to interview, communicate and take direction at any age. You need to take classes that give you the tools to audition, prepare for cold readings, commercials, approach a script and scene study, along with monologues, drama, comedy and especially improvisation.

There are an array of types of acting schools and classes depending on where you live. Again, remember that Google is your friend. Always ask if you can audit a class for free. Usually the answer is no. But some of these schools will offer a free seminar.

Let's start with general acting schools that are staffed by actors and actors who direct (you will find schools listed in the resources section). These schools will typically require you to purchase a package of classes for acting, modeling, singing, etc., for the purpose of attending a talent convention. The schools should promise that you will meet with Casting Directors/Agents after the convention or a certain period of time. These schools usually are expensive but may get you noticed. Also, an aspiring actor should start more slowly, for example at a school that does not involve a substantial commitment or a huge package in order to test the waters for adults and children.

There are also schools in which Casting Directors and Agents/Managers conduct the classes. These classes as a general rule are moderately priced. These usually are the most used by actors, with the promise they will get noticed. My experience has been that in order to really get noticed by an Agent, Manager, Casting Director via this route, I'd suggest attending these classes at least three times with the same Agent, Manager, and/or Casting Director.

In California, however, a law was recently passed prohibiting what are known as "Pay to Play" talent scams. The law, introduced as The Krekorian Talent Scam Prevention Act, was passed in 2009 and updated in 2016. It basically prohibits talent services companies such as Talent Agents and Casting Directors from charging an upfront fee for the purpose of obtaining an audition or other promise of employment. These services must also post a $50,000 bond with the state of California in order to teach classes or workshops. (See Resources for a link to California Laws Related to Talent Agencies.)

Statutes and legislation in other cities and states may vary. But when you do see a class held by a Casting Director, in New York, there will be a disclaimer stating, "This is for educational purposes only, not for bookings/work."

There are also private classes held by real "acting" coaches. This means they have had experience as a coach on a set. They were specifically hired by Production, whether it's Broadway or film to assist the director/actors (you'll learn more later on who Production is). Usually, an aspiring actor goes to a private coach either by the recommendation of their Manager or Agent (another topic), or word of mouth. Make sure these private lessons are someone who is accomplished. Again, Google is your friend and they should be on IMDB (Internet Movie Database).

Periodically, I am going to throw in some anecdotes of my experiences, whether it's something that happened when I was managing my twins, during my role as an Agent's assistant or even while acting myself. Here's the first one.

An Agent once told me to be wary of acting classes given by actors. This Agent felt that you could develop bad habits from another actor. I am not sure I agree. Would you take figure skating lessons from someone who never skated? In this business, you will find a lot of information that you must sift through and just use your own judgement. It is a different experience for everyone. I did ask an actor this question and their response was they would prefer to take acting classes from either an actor who has been an acting coach or a director. Meaning a varied background, which a lot of actors have because they do have to have a day job.

Finally, there are fine arts colleges and universities that have a Theatre/Film Department where you can earn a BA/MA in Fine Arts. These schools do prepare you. There are definitely high-end film schools such as NYU's Tisch School for the Arts, USC, University of Michigan, Boston Conservatory at Berklee, Julliard, Brooklyn College of Film, etc. But my purpose is not to be a career counselor. My honest answer is if you want to be on Broadway, go to a top Broadway show and look at the biography of the cast, even the chorus. More than likely they have a college degree and you will see that some of the same school names come up time and time again, as that is where Broadway scouts for talent. For film, go on IMDB, review an actor's education. The schools will be there, but they won't be as clustered as Broadway, or at least that has been my experience. Then again, there are also actors who went to law school, not fine arts school.

It's important to note that these universities conduct Showcases for Agents and Managers from film and Broadway for the purposes of seeking talent, especially for the graduating class. That's the beauty of attending fine arts college — you really get taught the business part at the college level. However, you will probably still need to take some moderately priced classes as, I will remind you, you are a product, and part of your business is to market yourself, NETWORK and expose yourself.

Again, I am not trying to scare you. But I'm giving you hard core truisms, so you'll know what is ahead of you. It's hard work, the business side.

Here are the differences for Child Actors, Adults and Retirees.

Acting Classes - Child Actors

Mom and Dad, the first thing I want to say is that acting classes are the greatest educational gift you can give your child. It teaches them so many skills that today so many children are lacking, e.g. interviewing skills, taking direction, communicating, looking a person in the eye, self-esteem, self-reliance, politeness and more. I am a proponent for acting classes for children even if they don't act. Personally, I believe it should be on the regular school curriculum, especially Improv classes. I would suggest an acting school, not a private coach, in the beginning so that your child is with other children in their age group. Sometimes there is a range, for example, 5-8, 8-10, 12-14, etc. Make sure it is a good range as you don't want your 12-year-old with a 5-year old.

Beware of scams. Be wary of someone coming up to you in a mall and saying, "I can make your child a star." Oh, how we all love hearing that, but usually it is an acting school trying to get you to join the school. Now, mind you – to be honest, that is somewhat what we did. We heard a commercial advertising that a big Casting Director from Nickelodeon was coming to a school and we should register for it. FREE. So, we thought why not? But I researched the school and made sure that it was reputable, and it was. And guess what? We got our first Manager there. This school made you finish a semester and once you completed those classes, they would bring in reputable Managers, Casting Directors and Agents for us to audition with at least once a week. After the class session was over, students were still allowed to come back and audition. It was a success for us and many of my sons' classmates.

Additionally, some of these schools would let the parent sit in on the class and observe. This is important.

Get to know the school, get to know the teachers. It's a lot of fun.

Again, you have Google, so research. This is a job for the parent of a child actor. Make sure that the school will connect you with Agents and Managers after they have held the classes. Typically, the school puts on a weekly show in which your child participates and/or the school invites Managers and Agents to attend. Make sure their Agents and Managers are reputable. Additionally, some schools promote conventions, which I will discuss later in this section.

Once your child has completed a package of classes, they then can attend the moderately priced classes for children, or a camp, etc., where they will get more exposure. But again, make sure your child will commit to the package. If not, you might try a local school that allows one class at a time.

Acting Classes - Beginner Actor

If you have not specifically obtained a BFA in Theatre Arts, do not fear. And even if you did get a BFA, I still recommend going to acting schools that bring in Managers, Agents, and Casting Directors. Again, if you have not been formally trained then look to a semester-based school like Lee Strasberg, Meisner, Stella Adler, along with the other schools that bring in Casting Directors, Agents and Managers (please refer to my Resource List). Again, Google is your friend. Also, everyone has an opinion on the acting schools that bring in Managers, Agents and Casting Directors. One way to evaluate them is to look at their roster and see who is teaching the class. Google and IMDB the instructor. See what they have done in terms of what shows they have casted, if they're a Casting Director, or who the Agent/Manager has represented. Sometimes these classes will mention a big Casting company that does big shows, but you are only getting the assistant to an assistant. Again, in this industry one never knows and the whole point is exposure and practice.

Acting Classes – Retiree

Initially take some Adult Education classes, especially if you are on a budget as most retirees are. They are fun and will give you some exposure. However, maybe you do want to embark on a college degree or invest in a Meisner or Stella Adler type of curriculum. Once you feel comfortable enough you can then attend the classes that are given by the acting schools that bring in Casting Directors, Agents and Managers. Please refer to the Resource List for more information.

Headshots

Headshots are vital once you are ready to start submitting yourself. A headshot is exactly what it says. It's a photograph of your head. A headshot should be taken from around the top of your shoulders and up. Because the industry has changed in recent years, hard (printed) copies of photos are not as vital as they once were, and you don't have to spend too much money on printing them. When my children were young, we would buy about 100 copies per child. Today I suggest anywhere from 25-50, as things are now electronically submitted and even when you do go on an audition, sometimes they give you the headshot back. They take their own photos.

Still, your acting headshot must look professional. Use recommendations and research the internet. Look at the photographer's website. Do they have headshots in their portfolio? Or are they an event photographer, e.g., Weddings, Confirmations, Bar Mitzvahs. Also, what types of headshots do they have? Are they multi-cultural and do they have both genders?

Do not have your nephew take your headshots, unless he is a professional photographer (again see Resource List). Headshots can range anywhere from $250-$700. This doesn't include comp cards for modeling, for which the entire body must be photographed.

Your headshot must genuinely look the way you currently look. The biggest disaster is if a headshot does not look like the actor. You may be wondering, *How often do I need new headshots?* The answer: when your look changes. I was once in a class where a Casting Director told someone it was okay that they had dreadlocks in the headshot they were using, *even though they no longer had them.* They were told to just tell the Casting Director their look changed. NO, NO, NO, you must look like your photos.

If you've gained or lost weight, you need new shots. If your hair cut/color has changed dramatically, you need a new headshot. This is very important because your headshot is what a Casting Director, Agent or Manager will see. If you don't look like your photo when you walk in that is not a good thing. Also take many different types of shots with different looks, e.g. in a suit, casual, athletic. For guys, have a headshot with a beard and one without a beard. Have a serious face, a smiling face and sometimes a silly face. Show your different looks, if you can. This is easy to do when you have your own website.

If you have any tattoos, that are visible (e.g. you are wearing a tank top or short-sleeved shirt) they should not be photoshopped out. Today, tattoos are not necessarily a negative and make-up can cover them if you get a job where they are not necessary.

When my sons obtained their first Manager, they each had tiny ponytails (which you could not see on their headshots). She actually said she would not represent them unless they cut them. Guess what we did? We cut them, and they were 9 years old at the time. Honestly, we could have pinned them back, as a Casting Director told us, however we thought it would be to their benefit to cut them off. Sometimes, these are the decisions you must make.

Don't get caught in the school game, where they promise classes and professional headshots for a large fee. Just be very careful of scams and poor quality as you get what you pay for.

Headshots - Child Actors

For child actors ages 5 and under you do not have to get a headshot when first starting out. Up to age 7, a good quality photo would work in some cases, e.g. modeling, you can "snail mail" a snapshot to a modeling agency and that is fine. However, once they are at the age of taking acting classes and ready for the road, they should have a headshot. As stated above when your look changes a new headshot should be obtained. Children change constantly. Under age 12 one can stretch it to every two years but I'd be careful. When puberty hits, every six months is recommended depending on how much they have changed.

People wonder what they should do if their child has braces. Braces are not a hinderance. In fact, they can sometimes be helpful. For modeling specifically, it could lower your game but not by much. Nevertheless, you should get another headshot with the braces or if you get a call for an audition definitely mention that your child has braces. It's very important that if you do have an Agent/Manager please let them know as soon as your orthodontist recommends them.

Headshots - Beginner Actor

There really isn't much to add except to again reiterate that your headshot should be a genuine representation of you. Of course, we all look better in a professional photograph, but it still should genuinely look like you.

If your look changes (hair length or color), get a new headshot. Men are tricky as men may or may not have a beard. I suggest headshots with both looks, and if you do have a beard, always say you will shave it.

Headshots - Retirees

If you decide that you just want to focus on Background Work (BG, used to be referred to as "Extras"), then in the beginning just get a few good quality photographs and post them on the BG casting sites. Make sure some are in full body. See Resources for a list of sites.

If you do want to get a headshot, you don't have to spend a ton of money, not yet. Go onto Groupon and more than likely there are photographers that have coupons, so for your first set that is a good start. But again, should you go further then follow my directions previously stated in this section regarding finding a good Headshot photographer. Again, you get what you pay for.

Resume

You should always have a resume. It should be in the standard Acting Format, not the typical business format. The Appendix contains a sample of the proper format.

Even if you have no acting experience you should have your vitals on it (Age Range, Hair Color, Eye Color, Height, Clothing sizes, Shoe Size etc.). Never lie about your vitals, e.g., clothing size, as this is used for an audition. It should show the skills that you have, including whether you have a valid driver's license. We all have skills whether it's riding a bicycle, dancing, singing, tennis, ping-pong, etc. However, do not ever lie and state that you have a skill you cannot perform. For example, if they are looking for a skateboarder do not say you know how to skateboard. They will test you on your skills and if you fail it does not look good for you. Remember this is like any job - if you lie about a skill and get caught, you get fired.

Also, if you've done local theatre or were in the class play, include them. Everything counts, even if it happened over 20 years ago. School plays and local community theatre are great to be involved in. It gives you excellent experience and it does count on your resume.

Additionally, it should list any type of training you have had. It should be specific to the industry. But there are some exceptions. For example, trained to be a chef, definitely include something like that. A major difference between a business resume and an acting resume is that an actor's resume does not have to list dates. You can put items in sequential order or by strength of the role or show. The reason is that if you appeared on a TV show 10 years ago, just by virtue of the name it will be known when it was done. Sections should be as follows:

- Name
- Telephone-but don't put address
- If you have a Manager/Agent their number should be on it.
- Vitals, as stated above
- Valid Passport
- Film/New Media
- TV
- Commercial-conflicts upon request
- Theatre
- Print
- Training
- Special Skills
- Volunteer work if industry related

Some of these headings can be combined, e.g. Film, New Media, TV. If you do have an Agent/Manager and they are exclusive, put their phone number on it and eliminate yours. If you are self-submitting to something and you are non-exclusive, include your contact information. (Chapter 2 further explains Agents/Managers and what exclusive and non-exclusive means.) This is why a computer and the internet are such necessary tools, as things change on a dime.

Resume - Child Actor

A child actor's Resume is somewhat similar in format, with a few notable differences. A child's Date of Birth must be on the Resume. Never include an address. Include the parent's telephone number, never the child's, even if they have a cell phone. Should you get an Agent/Manager then their number should be there. Some Agents/Managers do not want the parent's telephone number on the Resume. That is something you should discuss when speaking with one. (More on the Agent/Manager relationship will be discussed in Chapter 2 of this Guidebook.)

Do put on the Child Actor's Resume that they have their acting working papers, including which state and the expiration date (this will be addressed in further detail in Chapter 3). Every state has a different process. But a child actor must have them, and it is best that they are up to date. Additionally, if your child has a passport that is a major plus and list that on the Resume too.

Resume - Beginner Actor

Again, if you are just starting out follow what I previously stated. However, in order to get experience and a reel the best way to start out is to do student films. Additionally, there is a lot of non-union work which is a great place to start and perhaps even stay. It is a choice.

Resume – Retiree

Not much to add except you may be able to re-purpose some of your skills to acting. For example, maybe you were a teacher or an executive that gave presentations. You can add that as a special skill. Ask yourself questions and you may find that your previous jobs can apply.

Prepare - Conclusion

The last thing I would like to mention in this chapter is that, as with anything, technology has changed the entertainment industry on the actors' business side. Remember, you are a product and you have to market yourself. Having a website is a great thing, but in the beginning many of the casting sites enable you to create a website. So, before you become famous, use that service and put the link on your Resume. You can put your headshots on it, voice over demos and even reels. More on marketing later.

Chapter 2 – The Cast of Characters and How the Process Works

Here are a few of the crucial roles involved in the production of Film, TV, New Media, Commercials, Theatre, etc. You will encounter each of these individuals throughout your career.

- Writer
- Producer/Executive Producer ($$) (And film distributors)
- Director
- Casting Director
- Agents/Managers
- Talent – YOU

Writer, Producer, Executive Producer, Film Distributor

The following descriptions are somewhat generic and explained in simple terms as this guide is not intended to delve into the production part.

But how does this all start? For each segment of the industry, whether it's Film, TV, New Media, Commercials or Theatre, the process varies but not by much. This chapter focuses on Film, TV, New Media and Commercials. The cast of characters does vary, especially in the commercial industry, which I will also address.

Again, this is in extremely simplistic terms. It all starts with a writer's idea, which then gets presented to a Producer. The Producer funds the project, along with the Executive Producer. However, the Producers need to find a Film Distributor who is responsible for all of the marketing of the film. However, they are all the "money," and all receive a percentage of profits.

Once these people get together, they need a Director. Again, this is the abridged version. However usually Writers, Producers, Directors, and even Distributors have Agents — and the Agents are the ones who start the communications rolling. Or it could all get rolling over a drink at a bar or on the golf course. A lot of times you will see the same Writers, Executive Producers, Distributors and Directors on the same shows, whether film, TV, New Media or theatre.

Conversely, commercials are different, and the process is much quicker. The process starts when a business has a product or service they want to market using a commercial for television or New Media (Internet). The business will contact an advertising agency which will then put together the Writer and Director. In this case, the producer – the "money guy" – is the business with the product. Film, TV, New Media and theatre do not use advertising agencies directly; they use the distributor for marketing who will use the advertising agencies.

Advertising agencies have the "client" to please as well as the Director/Producer as they are part of the decision-making process.

Casting Director

So, what happens next? Now that we have the Writer, Producer, and Director, they will need talent to implement their idea, whether it's a film, New Media, TV, Theatre or a commercial (which is usually written by the advertising agency). These people don't want to deal with the talent directly, so they hire a Casting Director/Agency to find the talent. But don't kid yourself. On the high end of the business, some of the Writers, Producers and Directors already know who they want to cast as the leads. Start looking at Directors and who they cast. Take someone like Scorsese: he has cast De Niro, Pacino, Pesci, and more in many of his movies. In reality, it can be almost like a job; when your boss likes you, he will give you more projects.

However, a Casting Director/Agency is still needed and again you will sometimes see the same Casting Director Name/Agency used by certain Directors/Producers. Why? Because they provide them with the talent they are looking for and, in the end, help them have a successful project, so why go with someone new?

A Casting Director's job is to provide talent to the Director to audition and then book them for their production. Casting Agencies usually have a niche in terms of who they cast, whether it's for TV, Film, New Media, Commercials, Theatre etc. There also are separate agencies for casting Background talent. (See Resource list.)

At the Director's request, the Casting Director creates a description of the part in order to find the right actor to submit for that role. This is called a "Breakdown." It has many components including (but not limited to) the following:

- **The Title of the Production**. It will also note whether it's film, tv, commercial, internet, Indie film, etc.
- **Date the breakdown is posted**.
- **Union Status** – union or non-union
- **Rate** – how much they are paying, e.g. Scale, $300 per day, etc.
- **Filming Date**- when filming will take place.

- **Submissions Due by Date -** the last date an actor can be submitted for this role.
- **Call-back Note/Dates** – when call-backs will take place, and where, or any other information pertinent to a call-back audition.
- **Requesting Submissions From** – this is the geographical area from where they want the actors. For example, if they are shooting in Philadelphia, they may request people to be either local to that area, or from the surrounding states. Sometimes they don't care so they will say national.
- **Audition Notes** – when auditions will take place.
- **Role** – description of the role and what they are looking for in terms of age, race, gender, possibly physical attributes such as hair color, height, whether one has tattoos or not.

The Casting Director usually will post the breakdown to services that are used specifically by Casting Directors, Agents and Managers (i.e., Breakdown Services) for which they pay a fee. Talent cannot get access to those services/breakdowns; only Agents and Managers can. However, Casting Directors may put them out with some other services, such as Actors Access, Casting Networks or

Backstage. With these other services, actors can submit themselves for the role. This is called self-submitting.

I will discuss this in more detail in the section on Managers and Agents. However, I do want to mention that sometimes a Casting Director will not even post a Breakdown. They have their go-to Agents and Managers and may just send them an email or call them and ask if they have anyone for them. Or sometimes a Casting Director or even a Director may have seen an actor for a role that was not right for that job but liked the actor anyway, and now has a need for that specific actor (could be you). They will contact the Agent/Manager. Again, I'll provide more on this topic when discussing the gray lines between Managers and Agents.

Once the Casting Director receives responses from either an Agent, Manager or Talent themselves, they will then bring the talent they feel will please the Director/Producer for a first audition.

With today's technology, the first audition could be a video audition or even a Skype audition. This new technology has dramatically changed the industry; previously, only headshots would be submitted to a Casting Director who would then call that talent or their Agent or Manager in for a first live audition.

Managers

In order to really understand what a Manager does, trying putting the word "Business" in front of Manager. The

Manager helps you with the business of acting and has fewer clients than an Agent (or at least they should). The Manager gets you to Agents, focuses on your craft, suggests acting coaches, helps with your headshots, finds you an accountant, or a lawyer, and a publicist — again the "business."

Recently, there have been some changes in the Manager's role. In the old days Agents and Managers were very separate. Specifically, Managers did not submit their clients for a job/casting/breakdown. The Manager would speak with their client's Agent and the Agent would submit the client. Today that has changed drastically.

Managers get paid (by you) for every job that you work, even if the Agent gets you the job (more on this later, where I discuss exclusivity). This also means that you *never* pay a Manager up front. Anyone who asks for a payment upfront is a scam artist. Some scam artists will try to tell you, "Pay me x dollars, and I will get you a job."

Currently, Managers are acting like Agents and can submit you for a job also. Years ago, it was not that way.

Managers are not as regulated as Agents. Once again, this is a business "with no rules." I recently met with a young actor who commented that you can go to five different industry people with the same question and get five different answers. Unfortunately, this is what it is and it's rampant in this industry. However, it's a reality in any industry, just not as intense.

When you hire a Manager, they get paid by the job you have booked. Managers can command anywhere from 10%-20% of what you get paid. Although a Manager must join a Talent Managers Association, they are not regulated by any state laws. However, an Acting Talent Agent (whether they are SAG/AFTRA or not) must register with the state in which they work and are regulated by state laws.

Let's discuss the contract you have with your Manager. There are different types and lengths of contracts for a Manager. Most Managers have contracts that last two years with an automatic renewal if either one of you does not end the contract. Some Managers ask for three years. The logic is that they are working to try and find you work, and the work doesn't come overnight. Managers do work hard, again because they don't make money if you don't.

Correspondingly, there are "exclusive" contracts vs "non-exclusive" contracts. A non-exclusive contract with a Manager means that if you find your own job, they will not get a commission. An exclusive contract means that even if you find a job on your own, they get paid regardless. This practice of non-exclusivity is more prevalent in New York City than in LA and other cities. You must read the contracts scrupulously. I can't emphasize enough – it is always a good thing to have a lawyer read over a contract you are signing with a Manager.

Additionally, if booked by the Manager, your checks get sent to them and they take out their portion and then send you yours. Sometimes production does send you a check; in that case you have to pay your Manager. I have heard many instances where actors have not paid their Managers. This is not a good practice, as word will get around and you then won't have representation. Also remember that the commissions you pay to a Manager are tax deductible.

A word of advice on attorneys: make sure that the lawyer who helps you is familiar with the entertainment industry. I am diverting a bit as we had a negative experience regarding a "film" contract, not an Agent/Manager Contract but I feel this is the best place to address it. Our Manager at the time (we did not have an Agent for this project) said they had a lawyer look over the contract. Because I trusted this Manager, I signed the film contract. Unfortunately, we did not get many of the standard requirements one receives in a film contract. We later found out that our Manager had a TV lawyer look at the contract. Learn from our mistake — Television and Film/New Media are very different so you really have to be aware and so does the lawyer you use.

Again, this is a business with no rules and always consult an Entertainment Attorney for any contract. Always do your homework, and remember Google is your friend.

Agents

Agents are the ones that should be getting you auditions and then if you book the job, they negotiate the contract. They have more clients and are focused on getting you bookings. They don't spend time on the "Business" side, hence Agents have more clients than Managers do. Remember that Agents don't make money if you don't book a job. Managers also don't get paid if you don't work. There are also different types of Agents: Commercial, Theatrical (film/TV/New Media/plays) and Modeling. Essentially this means you can have more than one Agent, which most actors do.

You should make sure that the Agent you choose for representation is a licensed business by the state they are in. This varies from state to state. As some states, like CA/NY have a specific category for Talent Agents and a state like Missouri doesn't. Do your research. You pay a Talent Agent a commission for booking you a job. The amount may vary, for example, if the production is a SAG/AFTRA film/commercial production, the commission is 10% for acting, however if you are doing a non-union production, whether you are doing a promotion, a live appearance, modeling, etc., the commission is usually 20% that goes to your Agent. Additionally, some productions will pay the commission on top of your salary. However, depending on your relationship with your Agent they may still want the 10%-20% commission from you. Again, this can be very confusing so do your research.

Agent's contracts are usually for a year with an automatic renewal, as mentioned with Managers. Again, get a lawyer to read your contract. Although Agent contracts are usually not as complicated as they follow a standard format.

If the job your Agent got you was a Union SAG/AFTRA production, and residuals are involved, they are entitled to 10% of your residuals. Residuals can come from films/TV and Commercials. Even if you decide to part ways with the Agent, they still get the residuals from the job they booked you on. However, there are payments you receive that an Agent or Manager are not entitled to, e.g., per diem, meal allowance, mileage, penalties, etc. This can get extremely confusing that is why I recommend always referring to the SAG/AFTRA contract. Technically the Agent is due from you 10% of your gross salary from a SAG/AFTRA film or commercial, even your overtime.

Remember if a production is a SAG/AFTRA production you can always read the rules regarding payments made to an Agent, even if you are not a member. You can be non-union and work a union production, but you *cannot* be union and work a non-union production. This will be addressed in more detail in the section regarding union versus non-union. However, if you do a non-union job the rules change; your Agent will only get what is in your contract and you will pay them directly. Non-union jobs are not required to pay the 10-20% commission off the top, which is required for union jobs. However, there are non-union jobs that will pay the Agent's commission. Instead of paying residuals, some non-union jobs give what is called a buyout; currently new in the SAG/AFTRA contract, some low budget projects are becoming SAG/AFTRA and they do a buyout (again, you must read the SAG/AFTRA low budget contract). A Buyout is a lump sum, instead of residuals, although the Agent still receives their percent of the buyout.

Do I Need Both an Agent and a Manager?

So, the big question is do you need both? The word on the street is, yes, you do need both when you have gotten a lot of work. However, in the beginning a good place to start is by searching for one or the other. Again, keep in mind that a Manager is supposed to get you to Agents and direct your career, whether that is getting you to a dialect coach or providing PR.

The Agent's role is to get you the job. You may be thinking to yourself, *Wow! If I do the math, I will be paying out over 30% of what I earn!* Well, as I say, something of something is better than nothing of nothing. Don't get greedy. Also, remember when Agents and Managers work together for you, sometimes they don't take as large of a fee based upon the project. However, it is very hard to find an Agent on your own, as well as a good Manager, whether you are a child actor or adult. Again, this is a personal preference, but in the end, you need that connection to get you jobs, whether it's an Agent or Manager. Yes, Jay Leno has never had an Agent, as the rumor has said, just like Jon Voight left SAG (before it became SAG/AFTRA). But these are exceptions.

Also, keep in mind this is a relationship. Someone may tell you that they have the BEST Manager, but that Manager may not work for your personality. You will have to develop a close relationship with them, so make sure it's someone you "like."

What do you do? It's the old, "I have no experience, so how will I land the Agent and/or Manager?"

Basically, you start out on your own. Put together a decent resume and reel by doing student films and then start submitting yourself to Agents and Managers. You can start doing this with some of the self-submission services which provide lists of Managers and Agents. Also, Managers and Agents do conduct classes where you can be exposed to them.

Do some research on the Managers and Agents to whom you are submitting or who are giving classes. It's also helpful to use IMDB Pro. IMDB — the Internet Movie Database —was created for the sole purpose of having a source of information about all the casts of characters in film and TV and what work they've done. While I won't go into the intricacies of IMDB, it is a decent source of information. But in order to access the detailed information, you need register with IMDB Pro, which has a fee. You actually can take advantage of a one-month free offer. Since eventually IMDBPro will charge you, I suggest do it for one month and then cancel it. At another time you can reopen it.

IMDBPro is used by Managers and Talent Agents for research, so why can't you? It gives you more detailed demographic information, e.g., an actor's Manager/Agent information, an Actor's details, Production addresses, and an Agent's/Manager's STARmeter. IMDB's STARmeter can sometimes seem inaccurate but here is the basic mathematics to it. Once a cast of characters has been added to IMDB, (including yourself when you get a good Resume) the STARmeter starts ticking. It starts out at six million and every time someone clicks on your name the STARmeter drops. So, according to the STARmeter, the lower the number, the better you are. When you're researching Managers and Agents, start with the ones who have a STARmeter around 10,000 or below. But remember – the lower the number, the better they are and if you are just starting out, they are not looking for you (sorry to be blunt, but it's true). They are looking for actors who are already established. Which is why when you do start getting work, you also need to put yourself on IMDB, but it usually has to be reputable work (SAG/AFTRA).

There are inexpensive classes where you learn a skill and at the end of the class you participate in a showcase to Agents and Managers. There also are classes where the Casting Director does bring in Managers and Agents at the end for a showcase where you can audition for them. Usually the Casting Director has a relationship with these

Agents/ Managers. That is still allowable, even with the Pay to Play law.

If you received your BFA then usually there are showcases before graduation that provide the opportunity to find a Manager/Agent. There are many different ways to skin the so-called "Agent/Manager" dilemma.

My recommendation would be to start non-exclusively with a Manager as you begin your career, whether you're an adult or child. But do remember this will depend on which city you are in. As I previously mentioned, New York City is rampant with non-exclusivity but not LA nor many other cities. Where you live can be a factor in your decision.

Research or just ask what the Manager specializes in, union or non-union jobs, adults, children, babies, teens. If you are not in the union, you go with a Manager/Agent that deals with non-union. Don't make the mistake of choosing a Manager that focuses on union if you are not in the union. Additionally, since there are more non-union jobs out there, don't join the union too quickly, especially if you don't have much experience.

When you and/or your child are ready, try to meet with no more than three Agents and/or Managers at a time. The industry is a small world and they all talk to each other. Ideally find a Manager first, since part of their job is to get you to Agents. Since the Manager can submit you to jobs also, you are not left in the cold. Also ask the Manager about the Agents with whom they have relationships.

Again, it's crucial to find a Manager/Agent that you feel comfortable with. Also, never pay a Manager or Agent up front. Their work is to get you a job. Remember they make money off you, just as any salesperson does.

One more opportunity I'd like to mention is the industry convention. People attend these conventions, which last about a week, for the sole purpose of obtaining representation. These conventions have seminars and auditions (for example, runway, musical/singing/dance numbers, or acting auditions) for actors, models, singers, dancers to perform for Agents and Managers. Some conventions are for all ages. The Agents/Managers will judge you and decide whether they will call you back at the end of the seminar and offer to sign a contract and represent you. These conventions are extremely costly, e.g. IMTA, iPop, MAAI, and others where you have to audition in order to attend. The cost can vary from $2,500 - $10,000 for three days to one week of seminars and auditions for the areas of modeling, acting, singing, and dancing. However, you may get representation out of this and there are also contests which you can use to enhance your resume.

Although they are valuable, I do believe that these types of conventions are more beneficial for those who live outside of the LA or NYC areas. It's not necessary to spend that much money to get exposure if you live in those areas, because the moderate classes I mentioned can get you that type of exposure. But don't get me wrong, I know many high-level Agents and Managers who go to these conventions (because they go for free) and truly are looking for talent. But the antithesis is that these high-level Managers/Agents send their assistants and sometimes they are not paying attention or are directed not to give call-backs at the end of the convention. Again, we're back to the "Pay to Play." As I mentioned before, even these conventions are under scrutiny because Agents and Managers sometimes get paid to attend. So unfortunately, it is also about how much money you can afford to spend. It is a great experience if you can pay for it, however if you can't there are other ways to get exposure.

We never went to these expensive conventions and know many successful working actors who also have not. What it really comes down to is whether or not can you afford them. If you can, go for it, as again, it's fun and educational.

Managers/Agents - Child Actor

The previous sections cover adults, retirees and child actors, but I do want to provide you some specific information regarding children. Some of the "you" in the above sections are referring to the parent. Remember, your child is not the only one getting reviewed by a Manager and/or Agent. Mom and Dad are on stage at the same time.

I would like to share a story that did happen. When my twins were four years old, our Manager sent us to an Agent. This was back in the days before cell phones. We lived in

Manhattan at the time. I did not know there was a Columbus Day Parade. Hence traffic was awful, and we were about one hour late. Not a good thing at all. The Agent met with the twins but reported back to the Manager that they did not like me. No reason was given. Therefore, they did not want to sign my kids. This is a true story. Thankfully we did find other Agents. There was no explanation, but that is life and we moved on. After that we were always careful. We would joke that there were cameras in the elevators, hotel rooms and cars we were driven in and we had to be on our best behavior, both Mom and kids.

When children are under the age of seven, usually the parent has to be in the room when meeting an Agent or a Manager. When the Manager or Agent asks your child a question, do not answer for them, cajole them or interrupt. Please do not be a helicopter parent. Managers and Agents, especially, do not like this.

Children in Film is a great online resource for parents of child actors. It was created by set teachers and details are on the Resource list. There will be more discussion on schooling in the section "Let's Get to Work," as children actors must be enrolled in school whether it is a professional children's school, homeschooling or even a public school.

You must find out how the Manager/Agent wants to communicate with your child. As the parent, you are who they communicate with. Even if your child has a cell phone, do not give it to the Manager/Agent. Additionally, some Agents want to deal directly with the parent, but the rule is they should be contacting the Manager first. Some Agents do it that way because they are so harried that they want correct answers quickly instead of going through the Manager. Again, these are the types of details you work out in the beginning with your child's Manager/Agent when you get one. Communication is key.

Cast of Characters - Conclusion

It can't be stressed enough that "the business" part is where you will market yourself or child and keep everything up to date. Yes, you may land that Manager/Agent, but it is your responsibility to keep them informed on all ends. There is a term "Blackout aka Booked-out" dates which are the dates you are not available to either go on an audition or actually work a job. This is very important as a Manager/Agent does not want to submit your headshot to a Casting Director only to find you are not available. Honestly if this happens often, your Manager/Agent may put you on the bottom of the list or even book you out on their own.

Additionally, remember the term "Business Manager," as that is the partnership you have with the Manager, not an Agent. I cannot stress enough that you really have to be on top of your game no matter what, and that Agents and Managers work for you. If you don't work, they don't get paid, end of story. However, Managers and Agents want to make money, so you too have to be a "nice" client. As my Grandmother, who was a brilliant, successful immigrant businesswoman, used to say, "Kill them with kindness." Believe me, actors are a dime a dozen and can easily be replaced when you are not a high commodity in your Manager's/Agent's eyes.

Always be polite. Do not call your Manager or Agent and say things like, "I saw this breakdown; why didn't you submit me?" This relationship, like any other, is a two-way street. When hiring the Manger or Agent, ask them how they would like to communicate and how they will be contacting you. Some prefer email, others text, and some do both. My advice is if you haven't heard from your Manager and or Agent for a few weeks, depending on how they want to be contacted, text, email, phone and say, "Hi! I am checking in to say, *hello*," and then you can ask if anything is going on. My advice is call bi-monthly. And never ask, "*Why haven't you submitted me for jobs?*"

Chapter 3 - Let's Get to Work

The following sections will describe what your "business job" is as an actor or parent of a child actor. When I refer to "you," sometimes I'm referring to the parent too. The parent is also the business Manager of their child. This also covers what the audition process entails from the business side.

Organization

In this business, you must be very organized. Make sure you have all the tools necessary to keep track of all of your information, calendar dates, telephone numbers, etc. Technology has made it much easier for the actor and/or the parent of an actor. Your cell phone and texting will be the most important tool for you to have and use. Email will also be important once you get started with the audition process. You must constantly check your emails and your texts. Use your phone's calendaring tool or use Gmail or Outlook for scheduling. There are all kinds of great tools out there.

You must be reachable at all times and you must keep your passports updated, and keep your resume and headshot updated.

You'll want to keep accurate records of your expenses because many of your expenses may be tax deductible. As per current federal tax laws in the U.S., deductible expenses may include things like transportation costs to and from auditions, meetings with Managers, memberships, acting classes, even haircuts. However, I am not an accountant, and you should always hire an accountant who is either a good business accountant or one who specializes in the entertainment industry.

You can also join casting membership websites, such as Backstage, Casting Networks, Actor's Access, and others (see Resource List). Don't join too many, though, as Casting Directors only use a select few. Don't spend money where you don't have to.

In the beginning, before you land that Manager or Agent, these websites will be where you find auditions. Open calls, which sometimes are referred to as a *cattle call*, are advertised on these websites and yes, they're exactly as they sound. A Casting Director, Agent, or Manager may decide to call one because they are looking for something or someone specific and new. You must show up at a specific time and wait on a long line. These are sometimes a great place to land a job, Agent, or Manager. Yes, you wait on a long line, but you need experience and practice.

Organization - Child Actor

Children need working permits in order to work on any set whether it's union or non-union, paid or not paid. Every state has different rules so find the information you need by Googling "Child Actor's Working Permit in "state name." Get all of this done prior to going on auditions and or seeking a Manager or Agent. They will ask if your child has a work permit and if it's up to date. If it's not, that could affect your child's chances. Managers/Agents want less hassle.

We always had our California and New York Work permits up to date. Also, remember your child's academic education is extremely important. A child usually has to maintain a "B" grade point average in order to obtain a Child Actor's work permit. This varies from state to state. Some of the information requested when completing the work permit includes the following:

- Child Performer Information: Name, Date of Birth, Home Address
- Parent/Guardian Information: Name, Home Address
- Education/Academic Status Information: School and GPA
- Trust Account Information: This is guided by your State (Work Permit) and SAG/AFTRA (see explanation below).
- Physical Fitness Certification: Medical form completed by your child's pediatrician in regard to their health status.

- Acknowledgement and Declaration: acknowledging that the information is correct.

Regarding trust accounts, some states will have you set up a UGMA (Uniform Gift to Minors Act) account so your child can get paid. This is a joint custodial account that you can access. Your child can access this account when they turn a certain age. That age depends on the state you are in.

Meanwhile, a Coogan Account, which is required by SAG/AFTRA, is a Blocked Trust Account. This means that 15% of your child's salary goes directly into this account. No one can access this account. When your child turns 18 years of age this money goes directly to them. Again, this is protection for the child from their parents and themselves, as the UGMA account can be accessed by the parent. A Coogan account is required by union (SAG/AFTRA) jobs. Again, you must look to your state to see what the rules are as they vary and sometimes you need both.

Remember to do your homework. It is your job, Mom/Dad, to keep this information updated and current. I also recommend that your child should have a valid passport.

Preparing for an Audition

Every actor should always have a few memorized monologues at their fingertips. These monologues should be around 1-2 minutes long. It should show a range of emotions. Sometimes you may get an audition where they'll want to see you perform a monologue versus giving you lines. Usually that is when you are meeting with an Agent or Manager. But sometimes even on a regular audition in some rare cases, the Casting Director may ask if you have a monologue prepared. So be prepared. Your acting school/coach prepares you for these things. If they haven't, go somewhere else. Every actor should always have two monologues and a reading prepared. Again, I'm not here to teach, but I am here for the business part, and this is definitely part of it.

Once You've Landed an Audition

Here are some audition statistics: for every 10 roles there are around 1,500 submissions. Around 100-150 people are called in for an audition for a role. Then about 20-30 people get a Call-Back audition. Remember this is for one booking. Just getting an audition is an accomplishment.

So, congratulations – you got an audition! What's next? Usually the audition will have a date and specific time. Whether it's from a website or from a Manager/Agent, you must be available. Be careful regarding changing the time, that is why you must always be available — actor, parent, child. Again, if you say you are on another acting job, they will try to work around that, especially if they want you. Sometimes they will even work with the production you are on, as Casting Directors know each other and that is helpful.

Also remember to get the contact information of the casting people you are auditioning with, whether it's an email or phone number.

If this is from a regular breakdown, without a Manager or Agent, you will usually get a pretty clear description of what your role is and the story behind it, whether it is a film, TV/New Media, Commercial, Print etc. You are provided with a bit about your role, so you will know how to dress. Nine times out of ten you are provided with your portion of the script, aka "sides," from the breakdown. If no sides are attached usually there is a number or email you can contact in order to obtain them. It's also possible they may want you to improvise or get the sides at the time of the audition (again prepare + classes). Remember sometimes this can be the day before. There is usually no forewarning, especially if this is an in-person audition.

If this audition is obtained from your Agent/Manager, they will get the sides to you. They will give you all the details as stated above. Your Manager/Agent will tell you how to dress, as usually they have had direct contact with the Casting Director. If not, ASK. You also will get the date and time of the audition. Again, remember you are on call and have to be available. It could be the day before or in fact, we used to get called the day of. Don't balk, unless you are on another performing job which your Agent/Manager should be aware of, because you have informed them and booked yourself out.

When you get sides, MEMORIZE them. Some Casting Directors say it's not that important. WRONG, it is. If you haven't memorized them make sure you look at the sides no more than 2-3 times during the actual audition. They should be held in front of you, so you can easily look down and your face can be seen. You never want to take eyes away from the camera. Again, this is not an acting class, and this is something you learn in class.

There are also video auditions. In this case, you get an audition and they want you to "self-tape." (I love that term, because we don't use either tape or film anymore.)

With a video audition, Casting gives you the sides (again whether from your Manager/Agent or Service) and you have to record yourself. If you have a Manager, part of their job is to help you to self-tape for free. Agents don't do that. Additionally, an acting teacher can help you. I highly recommend having a teacher to help you interpret the sides. If you are in a city like NY or LA, there are places where you can self-tape. Again, your acting coach or a service will charge you a fee but that's part of your expenses and the cost of acting, and worth it.

If you don't have a Manager, acting coach or a service this is where your marketing skills come in. In today's world of selfies, the technology has become so fantastic that you can self-tape from your phone. Even editing on your smartphone is becoming standard practice. Many Casting Directors will state it can be done on a smartphone. They will also tell you other tidbits, like using a plain background and many other things. Make sure you Google to find the services that will help you to self-tape in your area. Once you become SAG/AFTRA, the main offices have these services for free, but again you must live near them.

If you need someone to read the other person's lines and you don't have a Manager/Acting Coach or an actor friend, then use a regular friend. Realize some people in the industry disagree with using a non-acting friend. There are also some differences of opinion about video auditions and whether your reader should be acting or just be reading. Some feel that if the reader is just reading, you will be able to show your true acting skills, however I am not sure I agree with that. At many of the large Showcases, like IMTA where auditions are in front of Agents and Managers, the reader is very bland. This is to emphasize what you can do. I think the jury is out on whether your reader should show acting prowess or not. Again, no rules.

Along with self-tape, some auditions are being performed via Skype. Practice using your Skype account with friends and family. If you don't have one, set one up, it's FREE. I can't say it enough times, MEMORIZE.

When my kids were young, we had a clunky video camera and I learned how to edit the auditions and send them. They would be each other's reader. Back then the internet was not as savvy nor were there smartphones, as there are today. It was not that easy to send video files.

Due to technology, the acting industry has put a lot of the onus now on the actor. This used to be the Manager's responsibility, so everyone's roles are changing, even as you read this book.

Should you use YouTube to send an audition you must be very careful. In fact, the Casting Director should specifically ask you to put it on YouTube in private mode. This way only the people you send the link to can access the video. At times, the Casting Director has their own service that you use to send your video audition.

Some etiquette to mention. It is so exciting to get an audition, you want to scream it to the world. DON'T. Be savvy about it and see what is already on the internet regarding the audition. When my sons were auditioning for the film *2012,* they wouldn't even email the sides. They faxed them. Now there are more secure ways to pass information over the internet. However, even today, the securest way to send information is via fax (a tidbit from my technology days).

Now it is time to actually show up for that audition. ALWAYS show up 15-30 minutes early. ALWAYS give yourself an extra 30-45 minutes to get where you are going. If it normally takes 30 minutes, give yourself an hour or more. Always better to be early than late. I have heard that if you live in a city like New York, because of public transportation, traffic delays do happen, and you just call the Casting Director, or your Manager to inform them. Usually if you make it during the call times, they will generally see you. However, if you get there after the call times you more than likely won't be seen. Do not make it a habit to be late for auditions. Believe me, and as I've mentioned more than once, you are being watched, and Casting Directors, Agents, Managers all talk to each other.

When you arrive at the audition, there is a sign-in sheet with a bunch of information they will ask you. If you don't see one, make sure you ask where it is. Then make sure you fill it out properly. They will usually ask for your Agent/ Manager's telephone number. If you are non-exclusive and you got the audition on your own, then you can say you don't have an Agent/Manager. However, if you are exclusive or your Agent/Manager got the audition, you MUST put their contact information on the sign-in sheet. Honestly, even if I found something for myself or my kids (and we were non-exclusive) and the job was giving the 10% plus I would put either our Manager/Agent's number down, as it's just a nice thing to do. But that is a personal choice, since it's not coming out of your pocket. NEVER put your Social Security number on it. The form is usually self-explanatory.

This is where it matters the most to sit patiently and be extremely polite. I have seen people pace and loudly repeat their sides or just chat. Many times, the Casting Director will come out and tell people to be quiet because they are taping. Don't be the noisy or rude one.

Now it is time for the audition. Remember to be polite. Do not talk too much when you get in with the Casting

Directors. Usually when it's a first audition it is only the Casting Director, not the director. They will tape you. They may ask you to do the audition a different way, to see how well you follow directions. If they ask you questions, answer succinctly. Remember they are auditioning a lot of people in a small amount of time. When you are finished, say "Thank you." If for some reason they made you use props, make sure you put the props back where you found them. Walk out that door and forget about it. Really, don't start playing the "shoulda" game. (You can learn this and more from an Audition Technique class.)

After the Audition

It is always a good thing to send a Thank You postcard after an audition. Try to get the address of the Casting Director you are meeting with before the audition. This is when your Manager/Agent, if you have one, helps. If you got the audition through a service, usually the Casting Director and an address is mentioned. It is great marketing to send them a Thank You postcard with a photo of yourself and your information. Don't forget to say what you auditioned for. Don't say anything negative. Make sure your postcard has your photo on it and all contact information. If you are exclusively signed with a Manager/Agent, then you must include their contact information. If you are non-exclusive and you found the audition on your own, then you can put your number.

However, if a Manager/Agent found it for you, you must put their number on it.

Non-exclusive contracts are more prevalent in New York than Los Angeles. This is where organization is so important. Another suggestion is to get postcards of your headshot but keep contact information off, so you can write it by hand on the card.

Also keep track of who you meet. As an added marketing tool, you should send a follow up postcard around a month after an audition and mention what roles you have done since you've seen them; even if you haven't, just send one. Or mention some classes you are taking. Remember Marketing 101—you are the product and you should be doing it on a monthly basis. If anything, just remind them when they met you, even if it was a while back. You never know what shows up on a Casting Director's desk. My sons once auditioned for a Broadway play that they did not get but the Casting Director remembered them for something else and called us for a different audition. You never know in this business with no rules.

Auditions - Child Actor

Auditions for children are after 3 PM because technically children are supposed to be in school. If your child is reading age, 7 and over, you may be given sides for them to memorize. They need to practice these. Hopefully they've been to classes and they know how to practice and memorize lines. When a child is under 7, usually lines are not that important. Please note: if working on an audition is a struggle between you and your child, then this may not be for both of you. It is supposed to be fun. But if your child wants to do it, have someone else work with them. I was lucky as my twins had each other so my only role was to get them to auditions. I stayed out of it (well, not totally).

When you go on the audition with your child remember you are being judged, even as you sit with them. Try not to harass them and tell them to practice their lines. If they aren't memorized by the time you get there, then they are not memorized. Do not fight with your child in front of anyone.

Here's a true story. My sons were around five years old and we had a Manager who sent us out on an audition. Our babysitter took them on the audition. Late that evening I received a phone call from our Manager's assistant. She said that the Casting Director called her and told her that my husband and I had a fight at the audition. I told that assistant to call that Casting Director right back as neither I, nor my husband, were at the audition and that the Casting Director was confusing us with someone else. That was not a good thing and I never found out if this assistant really called the Casting Director back. However, it would have been beneficial to her because it makes the Manager look bad also. My sons and I used to play the "watching" game. When we were in a limo provided by production we always would say "someone is watching," even on an elevator we'd give each other the "eye."

You Get a "Call-Back" Audition

After the first audition there are call-back auditions, even if the audition was a video/Skype. So now the Casting Director and the director are narrowing down their choices. There is no set time as to when you get a "call-back" it can vary from one hour to weeks later. But in all honesty if you don't get one within a few days, more than likely you did not get a call-back. Commercials definitely are fast on the call-backs because commercials are done very quickly. But again remember, you got an audition.

What you wear for your call-back audition is very important. Do wear the same clothes you wore on the first audition. Perform the copy the exact same way and this time make sure it's memorized if you hadn't before. Don't be fooled! Memorize. Even if the copy is new as sometimes you will not get the same copy as the original audition, MEMORIZE. If you feel inclined, bring a trinket to the call-back team. Cookies, candy, maybe something humorous, will work. They remember these things.

Usually, the Director is present at call-backs and sometimes even the Producer. If it is a commercial, the "client" is also present. Again, this book is not a substitute for an acting class, these are things you will learn in a class. I want you to learn the "business," so after your call-back follow the same directions as stated above on your first audition. This one may or may not be taped. Be polite, courteous, and send a postcard after the call-back.

Sometimes you will get notified that you got the part right away, leaving no time to send a postcard. In that case, send a postcard saying you are looking forward to working with them.

You Booked the Job

You did it! So, what's next? Things will vary depending on whether it's a SAG/AFTRA set or a non-union set. Depending on what your role is, you should have a wardrobe fitting before you film. You will get the time and place as to where the fitting will occur. Otherwise the wardrobe can be provided the day of filming. Sometimes they will ask you to bring some clothes (especially if it is non-union). This is why you should be exact with your vitals on your Resume. Never lie.

You are told when, where, and what time to be on set. You will get the days, if it is more than one day but usually it is the night before. This can vary. It could even be the morning of, if call time is late. Remember, it can change on a dime. At that time, you will receive a Set Call Sheet, which contains all of the scenes and actors, production, etc., that will be on set and at what times on that day (non-union sets vary). It will contain script changes for that date. It lists all the addresses and telephone numbers of everyone in case you need to call. It even has what the predicted weather is and what happens if there is a change in the weather. Sometimes script changes are given to you when you get on set, so please pay attention to the call sheet and make sure you get the current one.

Another tidbit is that when there are script changes, the color of the paper changes so you know there is a change; it will not be white.

When you arrive on the set, the first place you have to find is Production and sign in. Depending on what your role is and how large the set is, sometimes you will get a driver to drive you to set, although usually that is for SAG/AFTRA. If it is SAG/AFTRA and you self-report (travel to the set on your own), you should be reimbursed for your travel.

Also, although it varies, you may get a trailer or a room where you change into your costume/wardrobe, keep your belongings, and stay when you are not in a scene.

Your wardrobe will be in your trailer or room. Please treat your wardrobe kindly. At the end of the day, hang up your wardrobe. Don't leave it lying around. Again, this differs whether you are union/non-union, whether the production is union/non-union and what roles you are playing.

You will have a Production Assistant/Manager (PA) assigned to you. This is your key person. They will usually be assigned to you for the duration of your job, whether it's for a few weeks or just one day. They will take care of your timesheets. Make sure you get them and sign out when you are wrapped (end of the day). They will give you the scene lines for the day. Please review them as your scene may have changed and you need to memorize the lines. Again, that is where the colored paper I mentioned comes in, but again still read and make sure you know your lines. Additionally, they will escort you to hair and makeup, and then to the set. Things may vary, as sometimes hair and make-up may come to you or it may all be in one area. These are important things to know so if no one has instructed you, always ask in a polite manner. Production is there to help you.

Once on set you will be following the lead of the Director or Directors. I am using the plural because there are Assistant Directors, Second Assistant Directors, lots of different titles but it will be clear to you what you will be doing during your scenes. Be prepared to sit around a lot, bring a book or a laptop, smartphone. Don't make phone calls on set nor take pictures. If you must make a call, don't do it on set, and make it during a scheduled break, as there are many.

You also will be provided with meals. Keep track of meal times if you are SAG/AFTRA, although this again is dependent upon the type of contract you have for the job. Everyone eats at the same time; Production eats first then principal actors and guest star actors. Background is always in a totally different housing, called Holding, which will be addressed in the Background Section.

Once you become SAG/AFTRA you should be familiar with the SAG/AFTRA rules. Most sets always have a

SAG/AFTRA representative there in case things are not going according to contract rules. This is where the difference between being SAG/AFTRA and non-union comes into play. If you are non-union, you are not protected. For example, they can work you 16 hours in a day and there is no extra pay and you could not even get 8 hours of sleep if you are working more than one day in a row. However, if it is a Union production, the rules apply, to the Production staff and then it trickles down to the actor. You could work a 17-hour day as a SAG/AFTRA principal or even a guest star actor but you have to be given 8 hours between wrapping for the day and the next morning call time. This is why the days start later towards the end of the production week. It can't be stressed enough that when you become SAG/AFTRA, read the rule book. Know your rights. SAG/AFTRA was created because of the industry abuse in the early 1900's. If you want to learn more, there is some historical information about SAG/AFTRA on their website.

Hopefully you are realizing that this is NOT a 9-5 job with lunch between 12-2PM.

Again, remember to always be on-time, kind, courteous. Make fans out of the various people on the set from Production to Craft Services.

Your Child Booked the Job

This is where the differences truly come in and you must be prepared. SAG/AFTRA, in my experience, really protects a child from not only the set– but even from you, the parent. There are things that need to be addressed and you as the parent must be aware of these things. SAG/AFTRA only protects if the set is SAG/AFTRA and if your child is a member.

Let's first start with your child's academics. Some of this was discussed in the area of Acting Papers and School Requirements. They are very important; you must not neglect this. In fact, as previously stated, a child usually has to maintain a "B" grade point average, but this varies from state to state.

If your child is first starting out and is in elementary school, you must be honest with your teachers and principal. If your child attends public school, they have to attend the school for a certain amount of days for the school to get its funding.

However, if you approach your school (principal and teachers) in a kind manner then you will get what you need – their cooperation in educating your child in the public school. Another decision of course is to home school your child or send them to a performing arts school. But do not do this before you test out the waters for this industry. Homeschooling is more prevalent now than it was when my children were acting. Private professional children's schools for performers are very expensive. However, in New York City, and some suburbs and LA there are public performing arts schools. Public or private, a student must audition for these schools. Another question for Google.

As it turned out, we had the full cooperation of our school district's principals and teachers. My twins' career started in grade school and extended through high school. I can tell you that when they were in elementary school, they were asked to participate in the high school drama because the play needed children. That was a great experience for them at the age of nine. Of course, that happened because of "word of mouth."

Subsequently, when it comes to academics there is a lot to know and you must know how to handle it properly for your child. Should your child get a big job that requires a "set" teacher, you can negotiate how many hours per week they will need the schooling. Again, you must research this also. There is a lot of legwork when you have a child actor, so please do your homework.

Usually before you are called to the set, you go to wardrobe with your child. It can be days before or on the day of shooting. For a Union set the parent/guardian (which can be anyone you have legally deemed to handle your child for that day) must be in the dressing room with your child for the protection of your child. We have been on non-union sets and I was always in the wardrobe dressing room with my children.

You must be on set with your child. In fact, if it is a SAG/AFTRA production you must be able to hear and see your child when you are on a set. I've been given headphones so that I could hear them.

If it is a non-union production, the above requirement is not always followed. One time on a non-union job, I was asked if I would allow my son to film without me being present because the set was so small. I allowed it as I felt a trust and it was fine. On that same set, a 5-year-old boy was working with my 10-year-old son. The 5-year old was showing signs of being overtired after working 8 hours. The Director suggested to the parents that their son should take a nap. The parents refused and said their son had worked 16 hours straight before and he was fine. If it was a SAG/AFTRA set, then the Director would have been required to stop filming. In this case, the Director did make the choice to stop filming even though he wasn't technically required to stop. As I mentioned previously, children have to be protected even from their parents.

We always have had positive experiences when it comes to working on a set. Here is where SAG/AFTRA does work to protect your child. One production had asked if our twins could work till 3AM. Since they were 13 at the time, SAG/AFTRA had to approve. I then received a call from SAG/AFTRA asking for my permission. There were younger children on the set and SAG/AFTRA did not allow those younger children to work. Since my kids were older, we were asked and of course we said ok. The funny thing was that when my kids were falling asleep on the set, the Director said they could stop but the boys wanted to finish the scene and they did.

Let's Get to Work – Conclusion

Always remember this is YOU or YOUR CHILD, "The Talent." You must be extremely organized. You also must be prepared for the highs and lows, which can cause anxiety and depression in you and/or your child. Be prepared for these highs and lows. You can do a commercial, be a co-star and then not be called for six months. This is part of the business of acting so be prepared. The highs and lows are very extreme, and you have to be able to handle that psychologically. Fame and fortune seem glamorous, but they are not really what they seem and may never come. I know many actors that do have "other" careers in order to be able to juggle this type of lifestyle. There are so many opportunities in this industry, and if you can handle the rollercoaster, it can be a fantastic ride.

Chapter 4 - Background (BG)/Extra Work and Stand-In (SI)/Photo-Double (PD)

Background work, Stand-In work and being a Photo-Double, especially in New York, LA, Vancouver, Atlanta, Chicago (or any city in which a lot of filming takes place) is a fun way to supplement your retirement, your acting career or even a good way to find out if acting is for you. It will give you an idea of how a set works and what it entails. This is also a way to see if this is for your child. I know many child actors that started out that way (although mine didn't and never did SI work either).

Please remember you do not need an Agent or Manager for these roles at all. In fact, Agents/ Managers do not even scout for these roles. You do not have to pay your Agent/ Manager a fee if you get background work even if you are signed exclusively with the Agent/Manager – but do remember that to some, background is not even considered "real work." I'd stay away from people like that. It is a great learning tool and does add to your repertoire as experience of knowing what goes on a production.

Stand-Ins are for the actual principals, co-stars, and guest stars. Stand-Ins are used to set up a scene for lighting and blocking of a scene before it gets filmed. The procedure of blocking a scene can be long and tedious, hence a production does not want to waste the actor's time so they hire a Stand-In to do this. They also get paid less money than the actor. Occasionally the Stand-In will deliver lines during the scene setup. The actors do a rehearsal and leave the set so that the Stand-In can understand the scene when they block it. Stand-Ins are not filmed.

Photo-Doubles do get filmed in a scene. That is the difference between a Photo-Double and a Stand-In. When you see the back of an actor's head, nine times out of ten it is their Photo-Double. The purpose is they are focusing on the actor that has the camera on their face.

Stand-Ins and Photo-Doubles are in the same category but many times they are different individuals for the same actor. Stand-Ins don't necessarily have to look exactly like the actor, but usually they have the same skin tone, hair color, height and build as the actor so that lighting in a scene will be done correctly. The Photo-Double has to definitely be more of a lookalike because they actually are used in the filming. It's fun to Google actors and their Photo-Doubles to see the likeness. Depending on the set, sometimes the SI/PD can be the same person.

Background or extra work is exactly as it sounds. You don't have to have experience as they are seeking a "look."

It varies as to whether SI/PDs require experience (see below on how to get this experience).

You should also be aware that all three types of this work – Background, Stand-In and Photo-Double can be physically demanding. It may involve anything from standing, sitting, walking, repeating the same motion for hours, standing on lines as a group. I once had to ride my bicycle on a beautiful day over the Williamsburg Bridge for six hours straight, but I had a blast. In fact, most of the time you are sitting around doing nothing in holding. For me, it's a great time and honestly you don't need much brainpower. You can meet some very interesting people other than actors doing background. I've met retired financial advisors, lawyers, teachers all doing background.

I want to also mention that many years ago Background/SI/PD were not protected by SAG/AFTRA. Today SAG/AFTRA protects these genres very well.

How to get BG/ SI/ PD Work

Getting Background Work is pretty straightforward. All you do is contact an extras casting service or casting company and register with them. Most services require you to upload a headshot and fill out statistics on yourself. These stats include your height, weight, size, eye color, your special skills and experience. Include your car if you have one as sometimes they will use you as well as your car. Keep in mind that there are cars that they usually don't select, such as white cars or most SUVs. A vintage, low end, or high-end car can sometimes help you stand out. You'll get paid more. Most of what is included on your Resume is what you fill out on the casting site. The most popular site is Casting Networks (www.castingnetworks.com), where the background casting offices list their breakdowns.

Breakdowns for Background Actors are for either Union or non-union. Every SAG/AFTRA production is required to have a certain number of SAG/AFTRA Background Actors hired on set before they can bring in non-union actors. But realize that once they have reached the required number of SAG/AFTRA actors they then go to non-union actors. In huge productions, let's say that 250 Background actors are needed; nine times out of ten only 30 of them will be SAG/AFTRA. However not all productions will follow the minimum rule, and they may call upon more than the required number. Please note the required SAG/AFTRA number of actors vary for the type of production. In order to obtain the correct number per production, you can Google SAG/AFTRA Background Actors requirements for a production.

Again, here comes the predicament of being Union or non-union. In order to become a SAG/AFTRA member you must qualify (be eligible) and for Background work it is the same thing. SAG/AFTRA Background/SI/PD workers get more pay than non-union. Union has more protection than non-union. There are all kinds of extra pay for a Union vs a non-union; for example, a PD (Photo-Double) gets paid more than the regular Background but a SI (Stand-In) does not. [1] Additionally, SAG/AFTRA BG Actors get extra pay for things such as a special ability (which could be yoga, figure skating, smoking, working in the rain etc.). They also get additional monies if the production incurs penalties, such as not giving meals within the allotted times. SAG/AFTRA members get paid automatically for eight hours at the rate established, whether they work four or eight hours. If you work overtime, you get paid time and a half and for anything over 12 hours you receive double-time. Should you work over 16 hours, for every hour over 16 hours, you get a full day's pay. Those are referred to as the "Golden Hours." Again, this could change so always go to the SAG/AFTRA site for the Background Actors Contract or just Google it.

Back to the dilemma of joining the Union or not. Yes, in my experience non-union will get more jobs, but the pay will be less, so I think it does balance out. Again, joining SAG/AFTRA is expensive and it is a personal choice. However, I did become Union as Background for the higher pay and protection. I have met many on the set who are happy they are not in the Union. Usually they're not individuals supplementing their acting careers, but more likely supplementing another career or just having fun.

You may find articles on the internet that state that you can make a living from Background work. Please don't take these seriously. Sure, it could be a goal but from my

---

[1] https://www.sagaftra.org/files/apr18_bkgrndigest_f4_1.pdf

research the ones who do make a living from only Background work are people who obtain "regular" background work on a show that lasts for years. I recently met a man who was on *Law and Order* as a regular background in the squad room for 14 years. That was amazing to hear, but again what are the chances? That particular *Law and Order* version ended. However, it's fun to dream and it could happen to you, or it could be a stepping stone to an acting career. My experience is that Background actors come from a myriad of careers, from retired to aspiring actors, writers, etc.

How does the process really work? It's not the same as being a principal actor or any type of guest star actor, under five lines, etc. Background work and casting is unique unto itself. Background casting is usually done by a Casting Office/Director that specifically works only on Background. The biggest and most well-known is Grant Wilfley, but there are others. However, most of these background Casting Directors use Casting Networks (see Resource list). Background actors are typically staffed only a few days before the actual filming. Sometimes just one day before. When you join a casting service such as castingnetworks.com for Background work, you register yourself to receive emails based upon your characteristics. You also can peruse the website which has principal roles also (although most major principal roles do go through an Agent/Manager because they have access to Breakdown Services). I would suggest looking at the website because as I have found there have been instances where I have not received emails on some breakdowns. Also, don't subscribe to too many Background websites as they will become redundant.

When you receive an email, you should immediately submit to that breakdown. Remember it is usually for the next day or the day after. Then you wait to receive a text via cell phone or emailed. Your window of opportunity is tiny, and you must be attached to your cellphone and email. Ninety percent of the time, if you do not respond within 15 minutes, you probably won't get the job whether you are Union or non-union. The Casting Director has less than 24 hours to fulfill their responsibility of getting background actors. There are times when you will have to be fitted because the production you are on is "period." They will ask your availability for the fitting day and the day(s) they want to film. In those cases, you do get a bit of a head's up.

Additionally, in some cases if you are Featured Background, the Casting Director will email you wanting you to submit a recent selfie of yourself so they can submit it to the Director. Again, you must respond quickly, as there are many out there doing the same thing you are. Essentially when the Director wants to see a photo of a Background Actor, the Casting Director will send out these emails, not expecting everyone to answer, nor fit the bill, so they will take the first people that respond and submit them to the Director. Again, this does not mean you got the booking for that production. Everything is timed. Should the Director want you the Casting Department will either text you or email you. Each Casting Director works differently. But it all happens very quickly. The Casting Director's goal is to get the required Background Actors in a very small window of time. Sometimes they will contact you only the night before, sometimes they do rush calls and other times they may ask you for a couple of days. They may ask if you are free and never call you back, so if your main goal is to get work then always get "booked" vs someone asking for availability.

Once you do get a booking, you will then be given all the details: the time you have to report to Holding, the location, ID you need to bring, wardrobe items. Remember that Background work usually asks for you to be dressed in a certain way, therefore you are providing the wardrobe. If you are SAG/AFTRA, you get paid extra for changes of clothing. Additionally, if you are asked to be available for a fitting you get paid for that also, Union or non-union. Here in New York, there can be many different locals. If it is within the five Boroughs of New York City, you will self-report to set. If it is outside of the five Boroughs of New York City, the production has to provide you a bus ride to the set where they are filming from a location in Manhattan. The bus will pick you up at that location and drive you to the set. You do get paid for the travel time when the set is outside of the NYC Boroughs. Should you be using your own car on the set, then of course no matter where it is, self-report.

My advice is that self-reporting to locations out of the five boroughs can be more advantageous for the set, hence to the Casting Director. So, if you can self-report and it is easier for you, then mention it when you submit for the breakdown. It can add bonus points as to whether you get the job or not. Productions prefer you to self-report as they then have to hire fewer buses for the production.

You've got the booking, now where do you go? Casting is usually very clear on things. I always double check as it's possible to get an incorrect address. They also provide you with appropriate telephone numbers in case you get delayed and have an emergency. Again, give yourself enough time to get to the set.

When you arrive, there will be signs clearly directing you to Holding for Background. Always arrive 15 minutes early, as with anything else in this industry (such as auditions). Time is money and you don't want to be the reason a set is running late, trust me on that one.

Holding is an area where you will usually sit when you are not being used on set. As soon as you arrive at Holding, go to the Production Assistant and register. You will need ID (passport is the best, but a driver's license and social security card will suffice – you must be a US Citizen or have the proper working papers or they will turn you away). You also provide them with the number they assign to you. That number is golden so don't forget it. Again, you will be sitting around a lot. The production is supposed to provide you with proper meals, water, bathrooms etc. However, I always bring my own food and water because you don't know what you will be fed. Spec out the bathrooms and if you don't have direct accessibility don't drink too much that day and remember (yes, the mother in me) to use the bathroom before they take you to set. Unfortunately, there was a recent set where people were stuck on a subway for over three hours and not allowed to use the bathroom, I won't tell you what people did. It did make the newspapers.

Technically this is how it works for Background, and SI/PD. The breakdown will go out and sometimes the Casting Director will take only the first 50 that submit. They may look at only the first 25 and not like what they see, so they re-submit the breakdown. Always re-submit to that breakdown. Sometimes they keep track of who they liked and didn't like so when you try to submit again you may get the response from the system that you already submitted to this project.

Background is a numbers game. It is not a living, but just a supplemental income and possibly a way to get into the game. Even if you're background on a show, they may only use you once for that season. This means you have to always submit to different shows. Here's another tip: if a breakdown comes out for a Stand In and they say they want experience, submit anyway. I have had fellow actors with no experience get called. I also have heard stories where a BG actor is on set and they need a SI so they call upon the BG actor. Sometimes a Director sees you on set and then wants you to say some lines. It has happened! Background work can be a segue into acting, but I would still follow my previous chapters for acting.

For even more detailed information on this process, you can visit my website (www.joannperahia.com).

Child Actor BG/SI/PD

Being a child Background, Stand-In, Photo-Double is a decision that does have to be weighed. My twins personally never did this type of work as child actors. However, I know a few who have, and I watched children on sets. Again, this is a personal choice, but it does give a parent/child the exposure to how a set works and it is experience.

In my opinion, should you want your child to do Background/SI/PD work, make sure it is a SAG/AFTRA set because they are extremely cognizant of child actors and following the rules. For example, I was recently on a set with a lot of tweens and the set was very conscious of their hours (children are not allowed to work longer than 8 hours per day unless the Director puts in a request to SAG/AFTRA) and when they were to receive lunch.

Background/Extra Work, Stand-In and Photo-Double – Recap

Background/SI/PD work can be a great retirement career, supplemental income for aspiring actors or anyone who likes the entertainment industry and has a flexible job/lifestyle. Background work is also good because you can do it whenever you feel like it. However, it also can be grueling as you do sit around and wait a lot and can work long hours. However, if you know anything about production sets, even principal actors wait around, but they are accommodated much more nicely. You get to meet extremely interesting people and you see what goes on during filming on a set. You get to see the Directors in action and the actors.

One more piece of advice: don't be a complainer. I've watched many people whine and complain in all aspects of my working world. Unless you are a famous star, whining and complaining will only get you a bad reputation. However, if you do see danger, you must speak up and report that. Hence being SAG/AFTRA for Background work is a good idea as if there is a problem on a set a SAG/AFTRA rep is always available but only for members. However, I have seen SAG/AFTRA members give notification to the Union for the betterment of the group even if many non-union actors were on the set.

Chapter 5 - The Honesty Test: A Self-Assessment

In order to truly see if you or your child are made for this business, I have created three questionnaires. Depending on how you answer the questions will determine whether this business is for you. As we all know, there is a lot of talent out there. But the biggest game changer of all is whether you as either an actor or the parent of an actor can handle all the business responsibilities. This includes the realities of the business, including the ups and downs and the "on the spot" scheduling that comes with the territory. This also somewhat applies to Background work but not in totality.

Even if you have landed a Manager/Agent, you still have the responsibility of marketing, video auditioning, paperwork, scheduling, etc., whether you are the actor or the parent of an actor. It takes a lot a lot of hard work and determination and I am not just talking about the craft. Especially in this world of technology, the industry has changed tremendously. In the old days you would "pound the pavement" and submit your headshot/resume via snail mail or you delivered it directly. Today with the internet, not only do you need your headshot/resume, but you also should have reels, demos, and websites of your work.

There's much more to it, as you have learned from the previous chapters.

However, I created these questionnaires for the purposes of determining what is to come and whether you are prepared and are up to the task.

I did not create these to discourage you – they are to encourage you. These are personal tests, no one sees the answers except you. The key is to be honest with yourself before embarking on a business with no rules.

For parents there are two tests, one about yourself and one about your child. For the adult there is only one questionnaire. Again, you must be totally honest with yourself when answering.

After the questionnaires I will tell you how to score your answers.

In addition, I am offering a free 30-minute review of the questionnaires with me, for anyone who has purchased this book. Simply email an image of proof of purchase (i.e., Amazon receipt) to author@joannperahia.com and you will be contacted to make an appointment.

Adult Questionnaire

Consider each question and answer truthfully. Write Y (Yes) or N (No) on the line next to the question.

1. Can you afford acting classes, headshots, a website, social media? ____

2. Are you extremely organized? ____

3. Do you have the means to market yourself? (via computer, social media, mailings, etc.) ____

4. Do you have a full-time job? ____

5. Can you drop things at a moment's notice for an audition? ____

6. Do you deal with rejection well? ____

Parent Questionnaire

Answer each question thoughtfully and honestly. Write Yes (Y) or No (N) on the line next to the question.

1. Can you afford Acting Classes for your child? (children over the age of 7) __

2. Are you extremely organized? __

3. Do you have the means to market your child? (using the computer/MS Office, internet, etc.) __

4. Does your child listen to you? ___

5. Do you have a full-time job? ___

6. Can you drop things at a moment's notice for an audition for your child or have someone on call to do it for you? ___

7. When another person asks your child a question, do you answer for your child? ___

8. Do you deal with rejection well? ___

9. Do you handle it well when your child is rejected? ___

10. Do you have a calm relationship with your child in public? ___

11. Is your child a good student? (6th grade and up) ___

12. Do you know when your child is overtired? ___

13. If your child is overtired are you able to stop the activity without a meltdown? And can you calm a meltdown quickly. ___

14. When a teacher upsets your child do you confront the teacher? ___

Child Personality Questionnaire for Parent to Answer

Answer each question honestly and thoughtfully, and then write Y (Yes) or N (No) on the line next to the question.

1. Does your child actively seek out other children to play with? __

2. Is your child good company for themselves? Can they play independently? Do they make up games themselves? Do they play act by themselves? __

3. Do they enjoy reading aloud? (2nd grade and up) __

4. Is your child patient? __

5. Is he/she a clown? __

6. Is your child energetic? __

7. Can your child tolerate rejection? (over age 7) __

8. Does your child mimic other people in a fun way? __

9. Is your child comfortable with adults? __

10. Does your child relate easily to other children? __

11. Can your child easily carry on a conversation with an adult? __

12. Does your child have a good attention span? __

13. Does your child respond well to new situations or do they get scared, angry or upset and run away, get timid? __

14. Is your child outgoing? __

15. Does your child listen to you? __

16. Does your child listen to other adults? __

17. Does your child have a good attitude? __

18. Does your child want to act? (On stage, commercials, film, or video) __

19. Does your child have good grades? __

20. Does your child cry if they do not get their way? Can you calm them easily if they are crying? __

Scoring – Adult Questionnaire

If you answered more than one question with a NO, then you also have to review which question that is. If you answered Question 5 with a NO then you have to really evaluate whether you want to do this, as when it comes to acting you must be available for auditions because there is always someone next in line.

Scoring - Parent Questionnaire

If you've answered 7 or more questions YES, you are a go. However, the YES answers must include questions 4, 6, and 12.

Scoring – Child Questionnaire by Parent

If you've answered YES to more than 11 questions, that's a good thing. However, these YES answers must cover questions 7, 11, 12, 13, 16, 18, and 20.

I offer a seminar on these questions and what they really mean. Again, I am offering a free review of this questionnaire with the purchase of this book. Simply email a photo or image of your Amazon receipt to author@joannperahia.com and you will be contacted.

Appendix 1 – Resource Recommendation List

Acting Classes- New York City Metro Area

Bob Luke Studios. NY. Private acting coach and casting consultant. www.boblukestudios.com

The Lee Strasberg Theatre & Film Institute. This is probably one of the better, more expensive acting schools as an alternative to a BFA. Even BFA graduates should attend this school. www.methodactingstrasberg.com

One on One. You have to pay for an audition, but then classes are inexpensive. www.oneononenyc.com

Actors Connection. www.actorsconnection.com

The Network, NYC. www.thenetworknyc.com

Actors Technique. For Child Actors. www.actorstechniqueny.com

Stella Adler. A more expensive and intensive experience. www.stellaadler.com

Actors Garage. In Manhasset, NY. www.actorsgarage.com

IMTA. The International Modeling and Talent Association. www.imta.com/talent-training-centers.php

Headshots – Printing

Joseph Michael. This photographer will come to your house. Located in the New York Metro area. www.josephmichael.com

Vistaprint. Reasonably priced online printer for postcards and business cards. www.vistaprint.com

Reproductions. www.reproductions.com

Casting Websites and Related Information

Casting Networks. BG, SI and principal work, monthly fee from $9.99 - $14.00. home.castingnetworks.com

Central Casting. You register, there are no fees; they focus on Background work. www.centralcasting.com/ny/register

Backstage. Monthly fee for all types of work, more non-union, lots of student films. www.backstage.com

Actors Access. This is used by Agents and Managers; pay by submission; sometimes there are local breakdowns. www.actorsaccess.com/

Grant Wilfley Casting. They do most of the Background Casting for major TV and Film. You can register with them for free. www.gwcinyc.com/

Casting Frontier. https://castingfrontier.com/

Internet Movie Database. A good source of information on productions, Casting Directors, Agents, Manager. There are both paid and free versions. It can be worthwhile to just join for a few months, however when you get an IMDB project you should register yourself/your child. www.IMDB.com, www.pro.imdb.com.

Breakdown Services. This website is really for the Agents and Managers who pay large fees for it. This is where the Casting Directors list breakdowns for roles. Its sister websites are Actors Access, Ecocast and Showfax. Ecocast is where talent can send video auditions. Showfax is where the sides are for a particular breakdown. However, this website has an enormous amount of information regarding the industry and all affiliated services. www.breakdownservices.com

Child Actor Resources
Children in Film. The best resource for child actors, especially those just starting out. www.childreninfilm.com/

A Minor Consideration. A website for child actors created by Paul Petersen, who was a child actor on the Donna Reed show. http://aminorconsideration.org/

Child performer working permit. Each state will have their own guidelines and process. When you're looking to obtain a performer's working permit for your child, simply search in Google as follows: child [state name] performer working permit (e.g., "California child performer working permit," or "Georgia child performer working permit." You will generally find the exact state website you'll need.

Professional Children's School. www.pcs-nyc.org/

Industry News and Other Information

Backstage. Among other information, this site mentions apps you can download to help you memorize lines. www.backstage.com/advice-for-actors/backstage-experts/3-fastest-ways-memorize-lines

California Laws Relating to Talent Agency. Here are links to California's recent changes to laws affecting Advance Fee Talent Services.

https://www.dir.ca.gov/DLSE/2009Legislation-afrts.html
https://www.dir.ca.gov/dlse/talent/talent_laws_relating_to_talent_agencies.pdf

Deadline Hollywood. Online entertainment industry news. Also includes an entertainment business section and information. www.deadline.com

Variety. A longstanding entertainment news publication. www.variety.com

Appendix 2 -Tips for After You've Booked a Job

Information for Parents of Child Actors

1. Do they have 20 hours of school per week? Sometimes your child could be in a classroom with other children. However, they should not be more than four grades apart.
2. Interview the set teacher and learn what their background is. Always have consistency with the set teacher.
3. Make sure set teacher can work the hours you want and overtime. Be careful that they don't have so many commitments that they can't focus on your child.
4. Make sure you negotiate a minimum of 20 hours with the ability to get a few more.
5. Make sure you keep track of working hours and school hours to compare to pay sheet.
6. If in public school, make sure the curriculum is given ahead of time. This will usually be done by your guidance counselor or even the Principal, depending on what grade your child is in.
7. Negotiate exercise in the contract – this should be included in the school day, if not then there should be the ability to go to gym, have tennis lessons, etc.

8. Make sure you know the film schedule with regards to your child's school schedule. Will there be two different filming locations? Make sure there is consistency with the set teacher if separate locations.
9. Negotiate trailers if you can and make them separate from other children (for jobs over two weeks long).
10. Negotiate a set cell phone for the parent.
11. Make sure there is internet/Wi-Fi.
12. Always bring reading books on set for you and your child.
13. If not on location and in New York, make sure you get transportation planned properly and included in daily hours. Parking paid for, gas, tolls, use of own car vs production picking up.
14. Make sure you can get copies of pay and make sure direct deposit is set up immediately.
15. When on location negotiate a car.
16. Negotiate copies of scenes for reels.
17. Do not be a Hollywood parent/actor.
18. Always be 15 minutes early for pickup – be nice to transport and AD, wardrobe, make up.
19. First thing on set: contact AD (production) for signing in. Get into wardrobe: head over to hair and makeup.
20. Do not let them take advantage with overtime hours or going beyond the time.

21. Can negotiate premiere tickets.
22. Only complain when absolutely necessary. Wait till you're a big star to bitch and moan and even then, BE CAREFUL.
23. Read the SAG/AFTRA rules fully, there are many things the Agent/Manager can negotiate for the contract – don't forget it is illegal for a Manager or an Agent to take fees from your per diem (per diem is usually on sets that last over 2 weeks where you get a cash stipend for meals)
24. Have an Entertainment Attorney review your contract. There are many items your Agent/Manager should be able to negotiate within reason.

Information for Actors

1. Do you get a trailer or separate dressing room?
2. Set cell phone – if job is more than 2 weeks.
3. Wi-Fi
4. Always bring reading books on set or iPad. Phones can be interpreted negatively so be careful even though we are all attached to our mobile/smart phones.
5. If not on location and in New York, make sure you get transportation planned properly included in daily hours. Parking paid for, gas, tolls, use of own car versus production picking up. And find out how they reimburse you for it.
6. Make sure you can get copies of pay and make sure direct deposit is set up immediately.
7. On location negotiate a car/driver, if possible.
8. Can negotiate premiere tickets, if film and you are a principal/Co-star, not a 5 line and under.
9. Read the SAG/AFTRA rules fully, there are many things that your Agent/Manager can negotiate for the contract–don't forget it is illegal for a Manager/Agent to take a percentage of your per diem rate.
10. Negotiate copies of scenes for reels.

Appendix 3 – Sample Resume

555-555-1212   ***Wanna B. Actor***   VITALS

Email: SAG/AFTRA, etc   Ht/Wt/Hair/Eye Color,
                                                                 Sizes
Yours, Parent or
Manager/Agent info   **DOB (Child) or Age Range if over 18**

                                  Valid Passport
                               Valid Driver's License

Film/New Media

   Title   Role   Director/Production

Television

   Title   Role   Director/Production

Theatre

   Title   Role   Director/Production

Commercial

   Conflicts Upon Request

Print

   Description,

Training

   This should be all training /education that is related to the Entertainment Industry, you may include a college degree if it was a theater arts but it might be more
useful under your name at the top.

Special Skills

   Any special skill you have whether you can drive a motorcycle or ride a unicycle.
In the BG work arena, smoking is a special skill.

Volunteer Work

   Any related Volunteer work .

JOANN PERAHIA

More from Joann Perahia

Don't miss the latest news, updates and other goodies!

Visit Joann's website at www.JoannPerahia.com

You'll find:

- Updated resources
- Newsletter sign up
- Information on seminars

Joann is also available for individual or group consulting, seminars and other consulting services. Contact her at her website for more details.

www.JoannPerahia.com | Joann Perahia | Consultant

Made in the USA
Middletown, DE
20 June 2020